"A Precious GEM: The Journey of My Shaping"

Author: Devona Boone

This book is dedicated to my mom Eunice Boone. May you continue to rest in peace and rejoice with the angels in heaven knowing your story will help save someone someday.

Eunice Natalie Boone
July 12, 1962 - May 18, 1997

TABLE OF CONTENTS

Acknowledgments

A special thanks to Sasha Ridley of Heart to Heart Consulting LLC. She encouraged me every step of the way. I thank her for pushing me to write through my emotions and to put my feelings on each page. This process was genuinely therapeutic and necessary for my complete healing. I'm forever grateful for her dedication to push me into my purpose.

Introduction

Who is Devona? As I sit here trying to think of the words to say to answer that question, I realize it took me a long time to get to a place where I know who I am. I'm also at a stage in my life where I can feel myself evolving into something that I have no clue of what to expect. I'm in a season of my life where I can clearly see how far I've come. I can see how everything is connected and how one thing led to the next. However, looking into my future and trying to figure out this new journey, isn't so clear. So, is it crazy to say that I know who I am but I'm also discovering a new me and that makes me nervous but excited? Well, that's me! I am a beautiful, confident, strong, intelligent, focused, determined, motivated, hardworking woman. I am an honest woman who tries to apply the word of God to my everyday life. I was born in a small city called Franklin, Virginia. Located only 13 miles away is where I was raised, a small town in Southampton County called Newsoms, Virginia. The population is around 310 people, and everybody knows everybody.

There was a time in my life where I did not believe any of those affirmations about myself you just read. Now those words seem so easy to say. At the age of 31 I not only say those things about myself but I believe them. I realized that my outer beauty doesn't define me. I started to believe in myself and realized I am much more than just my pain and tragedies. I had to shift my mindset to think more positive of myself, which changed my outlook about my inner and outer self. Each affirmation I believe about myself now was once the opposite. I once struggled with my self-esteem. I didn't like anything about myself. As a victim of my circumstances, I felt weak, helpless and at fault in several periods of my life. At a young age, watching my mom getting abused, witnessing her murder and even in my personal relationships, there were times that I was helpless and had no help or no way out. Growing up I always felt as though I wasn't as smart as others. I had to study harder just to be average.

Meanwhile, some of my other classmates would barely study and would do exceptionally well. I always had good grades although I always felt like it never came easy. As I got older, I felt stupid for the decisions I made. Like the choices of friends I chose, the relationships I decided to be involved in and the fears I didn't face. I haven't always been focused. I've felt so lost and confused, not knowing if I was losing my mind or if I even wanted to live. I gave up on myself and had no determination or motivation. There was a time when I didn't even know if I believed in God or if I even wanted to anymore. I grew up in church my entire life learning about God and one situation completely tested everything I believed about God at the age of 10. I was furious at God, myself, my family and even my mom. I questioned my faith in a God who could allow such tragedy in my life at such a young age. When I reflect back over my life while writing this book, I realize I have grown in so many areas of my life. I can see myself becoming even more in this very moment. I am not a finished product. I see and feel some things shifting in my life, and I don't quite understand it all just yet. Throughout my life, I have experienced many tests and trials. With each failure and each victory, I learned a lesson. There were some hard life lessons I learned through trial and lots of error. My goal is that as my story unfolds, you'll be inspired to start making changes in your life or be a help to change someone else's life to prevent the vicious cycle of generational curses, lack of self-esteem, shame and fear of change. I hope experiencing my journey ignites a zeal for change and healing. This is the journey of my shaping. As you may know, a gemstone is found deep within the ground. It has to be dug out, cut, and refined to become the beautiful stone that you love to wear. There is a process that the gem must endure before it's even considered to be polished. It MUST be refined. Without the refining process a precious gem may be mistaken for a worthless rock. This book is a journey of how I have been shaped into a precious gem. Continue to read on and go on this journey with me as I not only tell my story, but I bring life to my mom's survivor story that lives on through me.

Do the best you can until you know better. Then when you know better, do better.

~ Maya Angelou

Chapter One:

The Warning Signs

God sends warning signs before the destruction! Have you ever wished you paid attention to the warning signs? I often wished my mom, Eunice Boone, would have paid attention to the many signs we both saw. I even wished that I had enough courage to speak up and tell someone she needed help. I was a child who needed help but didn't know how to go about getting the help I needed for my mom or myself. I didn't know who I could trust. If I told, would things get worse? If I told, would my mom be upset? There were so many reasons I thought of why I shouldn't say anything. Fear was holding my mom and me hostage, and we didn't even realize it.

In the year 1996, my mom met this gentleman who would change the course of all our lives. They started dating and seemed like the perfect couple in my eyes. He was nice and seemed to love and care about my mom and I. He began to feel like a father figure. My mom was happy and smiling a lot more. This sweet, caring man quickly turned into my worst nightmare. He began to abuse my mom. First, it started with verbal abuse. The way he talked to my mom was very disrespectful and scary to hear. The verbal abuse escalated to the physical, mental and emotional abuse. The happiness started to fade. At the age of 9, I witnessed countless acts of domestic assaults on my mother. There were so many but I was only around for a few of them, and those situations seemed to last forever. I always thought, when is it going to end? How long will he be angry this time? How long will it take for him to apologize this time? One night I'm lying in bed, and my mom runs in the house, quickly locks the door, props a chair behind the door and turns the lights out. I heard her come in and I was up, excited for her to come home. When I ran in the kitchen and saw the fear on her face, I immediately was afraid and started to ask her what was going on. She tried to console me by giving me a hug and telling me everything was ok. As she pulls away from our embrace, I see blood all over her hand. Her fingernail was broken down to her skin and was bleeding badly. Then the banging started! It was the monster, my worst nightmare, my mother's boyfriend. He was agitated and was banging on the door and yelling. I can't even remember what he was screaming. I just remember how I felt. My first concern was my mom. I felt sorry for her. I didn't want her to hurt the way she was hurting. I went and got some peroxide and cotton balls to clean her hand. As he banged on the door louder, I started to feel afraid. I didn't know what he would do if he had knocked the door in. All I could think about was him hurting my mom. I can't recall ever being scared about him hurting me. There was a time when she ran down the street barefoot to get away from him beating her. I was told to go in the house and lock the doors, as she ran for her life. Once again, I felt fear for my mom and not once considered being scared for myself. I went into the house, locked all the doors as I was told and waited for my mom's return. I don't know what transpired but when she returned she had a few scratches, but at least there was no blood this time. However, one incident that showed me how deep in trouble my mom was in was... one day after school. I come home and saw my mom had a black eye and her face was swollen. It was so bad I was scared to look at her. I asked her what happened and she lies to me! My mom told me this story about a bee stinging her on her face while hanging clothes out on the clothesline. Even though I was only 9 years old, I knew that didn't seem to be the truth. I felt sorrow in my heart and even writing this chapter has me in tears. Imagine the pain of a 32-year-old woman who has to lie to her 9-year-old daughter about how she got a black eye. As a woman you want your daughter to believe in you and to see you as her hero. I'm sitting here in tears thinking about how low and alone she must have felt in that moment. Who could she tell, not knowing who to trust? Having pride in the strong woman she was portraying, she didn't want to seem weak. Maybe she thought she was protecting me or protecting the man she loved. It was a year of abuse that seemed like the longest year of my life at the time. It felt like time stood still, we all just kept repeating the same routines. One day they would be fussing and fighting. Then the next day everyone would act like everything was normal. I didn't realize it then, but I was unconsciously internalizing what LOVE was supposed to look like because later on in my story you'll see how our stories are parallel.

As time gets closer to the day that changed my life forever, more warning signs should've been heeded....

One night my mom was asleep and recited the entire 23rd Psalms: The Lord is my shepherd, I shall not want. He maketh me to lie down in green pastures: he leadeth me beside the still waters. He restoreth my soul: he leadeth me in the paths of righteousness for his name's sake. Yea though I walk through the valley of the shadow of death, I will fear no evil: for thou art with me; thy rod and thy staff they comfort me. Thou preparest a table before me in the presence of mine enemies: thou anointest my head with oil; my cup runneth over. Surely goodness and mercy shall follow me all the days of my life: and I will dwell in the house of the Lord forever. I was amazed, but at the same time, I was wondering why was that happening. This was her favorite scripture. She always told me to read it whenever I was going through hard times, to remind me that God will take care of me and he'll never leave me. As a child, I correlated that scripture with needing encouragement through tribulations. All I could think was, why is she reciting this in her dream? What could she be dreaming of? What tribulation is she preparing for?

Then a few weeks after, I had a nightmare! I dreamed that my mom was murdered. I woke up and ran to her room crying frantically, mommy, mommy, mommy I had a dream someone killed you! She immediately sat up and comforted me with a hug assured me nothing was going to happen to her. Her boyfriend overheard us and then says to me, "Your mom isn't going anywhere, I'm going to make sure of that." My mom takes me back to my room and tucks me back into bed. She takes a ring off her finger and gives it to me. She says, "This ring has five diamonds, each day count one of them and on the fifth day something good is going to happen." My mom knew just how to calm me down and make me feel safe. I still have that ring today, 21 years later. After my mom left my room, I remember crying myself to sleep. Even after her best efforts to comfort me, I couldn't shake off that uneasy, anxious, sad feeling. The dream felt too real. The thought of not having my mom scared me. At 10 years old I couldn't picture a life without my mom. Only a week later, after that nightmare, all of our lives would be changed forever!

Chapter Two: Natalie's Closet

I remember this day, Sunday, May 18, 1997, like it was yesterday. I just had a birthday two months prior on March 19th. I was on cloud 9 because I was now 10 years old. I can't remember what I did for my 10th birthday celebration. I remember every gory detail of the tragedy that occurred on May 18th. The day started off beautiful. It was a typical spring day. The birds were singing. The sky was clear and bright blue. I could smell flowers in the air and the occasional breeze on my skin. The sun was shining brightly but not too hot. It was a perfect day. I had no idea how drastically the next few hours would change my life.

In my family, Sundays are for church, this particular Sunday my mom and I didn't attend church. The night before she broke up with her boyfriend so I'm guessing she wasn't in the mood for going to church. As a woman, I understand how relationships will have you consumed in your emotions at times. My mom must have had a woman's intuition that her now "ex-boyfriend" may be enraged and try something crazy, so we stayed with a family member Saturday night instead of going home. On Sunday morning we woke up and my mom wanted to go home to shower and change clothes. Once we got there, she became busy cooking in the kitchen. Then there was a knock on the door. It was him….my worst nightmare!

My mom and the monster began to have a conversation in the kitchen. All of a sudden in a loud voice, I hear my mom say, "What are you doing?!" ....and then there was blood! This man grabbed a knife out of the dish rack and sliced my mom's throat. Immediately I fell to the floor screaming. My mom and the monster tussled their way outside, and I followed them pleading for him to leave her alone. My mom fell face down on the ground. The monster begins to stab her repeatedly in her back. His hands were gripping the knife so hard, I could see the blood gauging from between his fingers. He stabs the knife in and out of her repeatedly. He flips her over and continues to stab her. At this time, I'm only two feet away still crying, screaming and pleading for him to stop. Even at this moment, I had no fear for myself, my only concern was my mom. That nightmare that I feared was becoming my reality. I was thinking this can't be happening right now, this is just another dream. I wanted to wake up so badly. I knew this was now my reality and all I could do was face it.

After a slit throat and 27 stab wounds, he stands up and comes over to me, standing over me with my mom's blood on his shirt, his pants, his shoes, his face, and his hands and says, "You know I loved your mom"! He runs in the house and steals my mom's car keys. Before the monster leaves, he cuts the phone lines so we couldn't call 911. As soon as he drives off, I crawl over to my mom. I put her head in my lap and cried over her lifeless body. I even heard her take her last breath. (Even though at 10 years old I didn't know what that sound was. I thought she was still alive.) All I can remember was holding my mom's head in my lap pleading for her not to leave me. I had never cried nor prayed so hard. At that moment, I felt so alone. I was losing the only person who was consistent in loving me.

At some point, my cousin Alicia, age 16 who was also in the house went to go get help. She took my bike, and by the time she got to the end of the dirt path, our uncle was passing by. She stops him and tells him what happened. My uncle Daniel came to our rescue. He picked me up from my mother's lifeless body and put me in his car. As I sat in that car, all I remember thinking was, it's all a dream. But then I looked down at my hands, they were saturated with blood. I looked at my arms, my clothes, my legs, my feet, my shoes.... there was blood everywhere. I knew then it wasn't a dream. Eventually, the undertaker came and took my mom's body, and I watched as they rolled her in the hearse. My world felt as though it was over. I wanted to die with her. I remember sitting in my uncle's car waiting for more of my family members to get there. As more arrived one by one, I saw the sadness on their faces and the tears in their eyes. The men of my family were beyond angry. They all rallied together with guns, knives and anything that could be used as a weapon and went on a man-hunt to find the monster who murdered my mom. This murderer was on the loose and not even the authorities could find him. I was afraid he was going to come back and finish the job. I couldn't sleep at night thinking of my mom and thinking about her killer still being free. Looking back, that was a lot for a 10 year old child to go through. To witness my mom being stabbed to death, watching her bleed out, her killer being free, being in constant fear of him trying to come back and kill me or hurt someone else I loved. It was overwhelming!

Weeks later, someone reported him sighted in Franklin, VA. The monster was captured, but my nightmares continued. I had to face this man in court. I felt weak and helpless during that time but looking back now, all I see is STRENGTH. I had to sit on the witness stand and give my testimony describing what he did. I looked him dead on in his eyes as the tears rolled down my face. Sitting in court, hearing and seeing such horrific details was a hard pill to swallow. To hear them say the victim was stabbed 27 times with stab wounds in her hands, arms, torso and back. To see pictures of his bloody clothes they found and the knife he used, seemed to make that day replay over and over again. Majority of my life I saw my mom as the only victim. I know now that I was a victim and its okay for me to own that. As I got older I learned a term called Childhood Domestic Violence. This term is used to describe growing up with violence between parents or a parent and their significant other. For a year of my life, I was a victim of Childhood Domestic Violence. I watched in fear as my mom was abused. I felt as though I had to be strong when she was weak. I often felt helpless like I was just watching, but I couldn't do anything to stop such a big man from hurting her. After my mom's murder, I felt guilt, like it was my fault. I felt like I should have told someone or I should have tried to fight him. Maybe if I would have done something my mom would still be here. The purpose of this book is to bring my mom's story to life and to help someone else before their life is taken away by a loved one who is enraged. Also to help someone see their worth by learning from our failures.

If my mom was still here what advice would she give me? I believe she would first ask the questions; do you know who you are baby? Do you love yourself? Do you know your worth? There was a period of my life when I didn't know the answers to those questions. I realized it was time to start taking time to figure out who I was and learn to love myself. Embarking on a new journey of self-discovery taught me that, love is something that is cultivated. Some people are fortunate to have self-love instilled in them as a child, making it easier to love yourself as a child. Some people don't get that reinforcement and may struggle with self-esteem issues along the way to adulthood, even during adulthood. When or if you start loving yourself, you'll attract people who love you as well. Learn your worth and cut ties with relationships that are detrimental to your mind, body, and soul before it's too late. You're not the only one being affected by the abuse, consider your children and your family.

I don't believe my mom was a weak woman at all. Her nickname was Butch, so that speaks for itself. She could handle herself. My family often tells me how my mom would fight anybody anytime. She stood up for others when they couldn't stand up for themselves. She would fight her battles, her loved ones and friends' battles. Even in her relationships, she fought back. Yes! I recently found out, she was in several abusive relationships; I wasn't born yet, or I was too young to remember those. However now that I'm around the age she was when she died, and we both have had similar lifestyles up to this point in my life, I see how vulnerable she was. We both seemed to have a fear of being alone. We both started dating young, got married young and both suffered variations of abuse.

At the age of 18, she had her first child, my brother. Then at age 24, she had me by another man. She got married young, and that didn't work out. Shortly after leaving her husband she met the "monster" at the age of 32. She was looking for love in all the wrong places. I am currently 31 going on 32. I can understand her point of view better now. I never understood why she just couldn't leave the abusive relationship. I didn't understand why she would act as though everything was ok when we were around our family. I just didn't understand why she didn't want better for herself. I now know that she had a fear of leaving, not knowing how "the monster" would react or what he would do. I also know she was afraid of being alone. Wanting to leave but afraid that no one would want her or love her better than what he was doing. I have a better understanding of the choices she made. I had to live them myself in my own personal relationship. Even though I may not agree with her staying in an abusive relationship, I have more empathy and understanding. My mom was in broken relationships one after the next. She never took the time to be alone and learn to love herself to know what she was worthy of. By the time she made her mind up to leave, "the monster" was so enraged by her decision, he went crazy. He was very jealous over her and maybe thought if I can't have her, no one will.

I believe If Eunice were here to tell me today, she would say, "baby, you are too precious to allow anyone not to respect you in any form." Love is kind, gentle, patient, slow to anger and it should never hurt you. Love yourself first, figure out who you are. The only way to survive is to know that you are created by God, and you're more precious than rubies and nothing can compare to you! You are fearfully and wonderfully made so live and act accordingly. Don't allow anyone to steal your worth. Your self-worth isn't defined by what others do or how they treat you. Your measurement of self-worth is determined by the level of self love you have. It's all about how you perceive yourself. I wish she was here to tell me this herself, but because she never got to learn those lessons, I am the one relaying the message. I thought I learned from her mistakes what NOT to do. Instead, I picked up those same habits just in a different form. I had to learn those life lessons on my own, and it wasn't easy.

Chapter Three:

Lost in the Transition

Life after my mom's death was a huge adjustment. The first year, I bounced from house to house, trying to find a home where I fit. Some of my aunts decided to step up and take me in, but to this day I don't know why I didn't permanently stay with any of them. I wasn't a bad child. I was emotionally unstable so there may have been times where I talked back or was sassy but what child isn't. I was still in shock, trying to grieve but never really adequately healed. As a child, all I could remember feeling was unwanted and feeling like a burden until finally my grandmother stepped in and took me into her home. This wasn't a cake walk either. I felt as though she did it out of obligation instead of wanting or yearning to take care of me. There were already people staying at my grandparents' house. My grandmother shared a bed with one of my younger cousins, and another was on the couch. When I arrived, there was nowhere for me to sleep but a fold out beach chair. Sleeping on the floor was not an option because the house was infested with roaches. I feared that I would wake up with a roach bug in my ear or trying to crawl in my mouth. I slept on that fold out beach chair for what seemed like forever. I remember sleeping on it so long that my bottom was grazing the surface of the floor...all the elastic was gone! I can't remember how long it was but as I mentioned before, time was standing still. I was so focused on trying to survive day to day and keep my emotions from taking over, I was never aware of a sense of time. Hours felt like days, days felt like months and months felt like years. Sometime later after I arrived at my grandparents, I got my own room after some changing around had occurred.

The first two years following my mom's murder, I don't remember many specific details. My body's way of coping with this transition was to block out many of those memories. I do remember the feelings or emotions I had during those times. I often thought about my mom. I thought maybe if I prayed hard enough she would come back. After a while I gave up on that idea, I knew she wasn't coming back. I began to feel angry at "the monster" who took her from me. I was even angry at God for allowing this to happen to my mom. I would look at my cousins and envy their relationship with their mothers. I thought, why can't someone love me unconditionally. When you hear the saying, "There's no other love like a mother's love," that is so true. No one could replace the way she made me feel. I felt safe and taken care of, and I haven't felt that since the day she died. Holidays and birthdays were the worst for me. My family is BIG...everybody had somebody. All my cousins still had their mom, and everybody seemed to be happy with their family, and here I am at the ages of 10 through 12, feeling as though I had no one. I was sad, depressed, lonely and even had suicidal thoughts. I wanted my mom, but I knew there was no way of ever getting her back. This was another moment in my life where I felt like a victim. The only person who genuinely loved me and took care of me was taken from me. I felt like I was left to fend for myself. I was responsible for my own well-being at the tender age of 10. Some people were there but not really there. My aunts stepped in and did what they could do when they could. I would run out of personal hygiene items, and no one seemed to care. I would run out of clean clothes, and no one seemed to care. I would be hungry, and no one seemed to care, or everyone assumed someone else had that responsibility. Now as an adult I think back and maybe I could have just spoken up but my mom always made sure I had the things I needed and I never had to say anything. Maybe it wasn't that my family didn't care, maybe they just didn't know and it was a new adjustment for us all. I quickly learned that I was the only person I could really depend on. I started making a list of all the items I needed and started buying my own personal items and washing my own clothes. I even brought myself snacks and hid them in my room. I know you're wondering where did I get money from. I received an SSI check which was Supplemental Security Income from my mother's worked wages. I received that check up until I was 18. While staying with my grandparents, my grandmother would allowance me $20 each month. She was old school and didn't believe children needed to have a lot of money. I would use that $20 to buy all the things I needed to buy. The Dollar General was my favorite store. I learned I could buy my essentials for a cheap price and was able to get everything I needed with the $20. I felt like if I didn't do it, there was no one who was going to do it for me. As an adult, I see how that molded me into the control freak and untrusting person that I am. It's hard for me to trust people when they say they're going to do something because I've had very few people to show up for me and actually do what they said they would do. I've learned to give people the benefit of the doubt. I try to trust people but in the back of my mind, I'm already preparing myself to be let down. Still, to this day, I have trust issues. I OWN THAT!

Before my mom's murder, I was a very confident child. My mom made sure I looked nice at all times and she always told me how beautiful I was. After she died, because of my appearance, I began to have self-esteem issues. I had beautiful long hair, which broke off very badly because I didn't have a consistent person taking care of it. My hair was so short I couldn't put it in a ponytail. My face began to break out with acne. I was always outside helping my grandparents work in the garden so my skin tone became darkened and I was teased for being dark skinned with acne. I remember being called a star crunch by a family member. I know they were joking but it didn't feel funny to me. I wasn't aware of the beauty I truly possessed within. I remember asking God WHY, a lot of times. I just got to a point where being dead felt like it was the best choice for me. I remember thinking, no one cares about me, no one will miss me, me being gone would make everyone's life easier and I was tired of dealing with grief. I didn't like my living situation. Living with my grandparents, there was no bathroom or running water. My grandfather kept gallon jugs of water filled in the kitchen that came from the well pump and to take a hot bath I had to boil water on the stove and then add cold water to my "washpot". I never really felt clean, didn't like my skin, my hair, my clothes, basically I didn't like any physical traits about myself. I didn't even know any inner traits about myself that I could begin to start liking. I was a lost soul.

My grandparents were very traditional. They had 13 children. My grandfather was a truck driver and my grandmother owned a small store where she sold baked goods or things she grew. By the time I was born they had retired but were hustling. They sold watermelons and cantaloupe in New Jersey and at the local farmer's market. They had 3 large gardens and a 6-acre field where they planted, harvested and sold crops. They were very well known in the community. My grandfather was very adamant about how important it was to get an education. He would always encourage me to not get involved with boys. He would say, "If you lay down with dogs you get fleas, stay in school and get your education". My grandmother was adamant about teaching me about hard work and having a solid foundation in our Christian beliefs. There were many things not permitted in a holy sanctified household. We couldn't play any card games because it was deemed as gambling which was a sin. We couldn't listen to secular music, only gospel music. We could never wear jeans to church. Before leaving the house, my grandmother would check our clothes and make sure everything was appropriate. I didn't have a real appreciation for those life lessons I was learning at that time. I was still grieving. I was still trying to adjust to my new life. My attitude began to get worse and I just started to hate life more and more with each day that passed.

While living with my grandparents, at age 11, they sent me to see a psychiatrist. I shared with an older cousin that I wanted to kill myself and she told my grandmother. I know now that it was a cry for help. I wanted to give up! Not having my mom, I felt like I was alone and losing my mind. I went to therapy for maybe a few months. I felt as though it wasn't helping me like it was a waste of my time. My psychiatrist used big words while he talked to me. I never understood what he was saying. There were days that I would go there and literally do picture art on his computer. I didn't want to kill myself anymore because my grandmother sat me down and taught me the importance of NOT committing suicide. In Christianity, we believe that killing yourself is a sin and condemns you to hell. She read I Corinthians 6:19-20 Do you not know that your body is a temple of the Holy Spirit within you, whom you have from God? You are not your own, for you were bought with a price. So, glorify God in your body. Then she read Revelation

21:8 But as for the cowardly, the faithless, the detestable, as for murderers, the sexually immoral, sorcerers, idolaters, and all liars, their portion will be in the lake that burns with fire and sulfur. After we had this discussion, I knew then I would never consider suicide AGAIN. I knew I didn't want to go to hell and I wanted to please God. I told my grandmother I didn't want to go to therapy anymore and she didn't make me go, instead, she gave me an alternative. She taught me how to fast and pray. I began to read the Bible more and she kept me in church. We attended Sunday school, Sunday morning worship service, Sunday evening services, Wednesday night bible study, Saturday choir rehearsal and then start all over again. If there were church revivals we were there every night. You think I would get tired of church, but I loved it! I found peace in Jesus and at that young age, I didn't quite understand it. Now when I look back and reflect on those times, I thank God for my grandmother. While I was lost in the transition, I had lost many of my material things, God showed my grandmother a way to give me peace and comfort and it was through him. If she wasn't obedient to her assignment to my life, I would have killed myself. My grandmother saved my life! I have learned that sometimes you have to do things you don't want to do. Just as I mentioned before that it seemed to me that my grandmother took me in out of obligation and not yearning. I believe that in the midst of doing those things you least desire, you may have no idea what you're doing. All you can do is give your best and rely on God. I believe that even in the midst of all the things that were lacking, she did her best. I grew to respect and love my grandparents even more than I did before. They took me in and provided for me to the best of their ability.

As I sit here, writing my feelings down, I'm reminded of Job in the Bible. Job was a rich man. One of the richest men in the area where he lived. He owned 7,000 sheep, 3,000 camels, 500 oxen, 500 donkeys, 7 sons, 3 daughters and a large number of servants. The Bible says that Job was blameless and upright. He was a man who feared God and shunned evil. There was no one else like him. God allowed Satan to test Job because Satan was so sure if he took all that stuff away from Job he would surely curse God. Everything Job had was taken or killed, all his cattle, his servants and his children! Job praised and worshipped God saying, "Naked I came from my mother's wound, and naked I will depart. The Lord gave and the Lord has taken away; may the name of the Lord be praised." (NIV Job 1:21) After Satan saw none of that worked, he surely thought that attacking his health would make him curse God. God allowed Satan to do this but didn't let him take Job's life. Job never cursed God. Instead, he said we must take the good as well as the bad from God. (NIV Job 2:10) In the end, God restored his health and fortunes. Job had twice as much as he had before. (NIV Job 42:10)

This reminds me of how I felt as a child. When I learned that story, I always felt like I could identify with Job. I felt as if God was taking everything from me. Although I started out angry after my mom's murder, I got comfort in knowing that I too can take the good as well as the bad. I can still praise God for who he is and not what he does or what he gives. My latter will be greater. I learned that lesson at an early age. Of course, just like Job I may get discouraged along the way and start to question why was I even born, but trusting in God gives me hope. Hope activates our faith.

Chapter Four:

Breaking Generational Curses

As I began to learn more of God, I began to understand more about life, my surroundings, and my situation. I found the strength to forgive the monster who murdered my mom. When I got older I even went to visit him in prison to tell him I forgave him. Once I arrived to the maximum security prison, I felt nervous and didn't know what to expect. I went through the rigorous degrading security search and patiently waited for the monster in the visitation area. When he came out, my heart dropped to my feet. To sit inches away from the man who brutally murdered my mom was surreal and I was flooded with emotions. I was surprised that he looked the same. I felt nervous, angry and sad. We talked and I expressed my forgiveness. He then proposed that I sign some documents to help him get released from prison early. THE NERVE OF HIM!!!! I immediately got up and left. I forgave him but I wasn't willing to help him get out of prison early. He did the crime, he had to do all the time. This was the beginning of a long journey of healing for me.

I made a promise to God that I wouldn't allow any generational curses to become my life. I vowed that I would not be like my mom and endure physical abuse. I also vowed that I would not be a single parent. I'm not saying that there is anything wrong with you if you are a single mom. Being a single parent requires sacrifice, dedication and hard work.

I truly admire any parent who has to take on that responsibility alone. It's just not what I envision for my life. As I grew older, I found myself looking for love in all the wrong places. Just like my mom. I didn't have a baby out of wedlock, nor did I allow a man to abuse me physically. However, every relationship I was in, was a world-wind of emotional and verbal abuse. I was lied to, cheated on, had money stolen from me, called out of my name and just blatantly disrespected through actions and words. I knew I deserved better but I lacked true confidence in myself, so I dealt with the pain. I thought I was loved because even after there was a break-up, the guy would come back pleading for me to take him back.

Surely, he must love me, I thought. I had no idea I was allowing myself to be emotionally abused. I was trying so hard not to follow in my mother's footsteps I became her. Followed the same destructive relationship patterns.

The vicious cycle of generational curses started when I was in an intimate relationship at 16, after a year we broke up. There was one too many broken promises from my boyfriend at the time who was a year older than me. He was supposed to come to my high school graduation and never showed up. I later found out he was with one of his multiple sex partners. Needless to say, we broke up, and only months later I was already talking to someone else, entertaining the thought of another relationship. We were friends for a year and by the time I was 18 we were officially dating. We were in a 5-year relationship and then married at the age of 23. I allowed the emotional abuse to follow me from one relationship to the next. I was determined to make the relationship work even if all the odds were stacked against me. I devoted myself completely in the beginning of the relationship. I forgot to focus or didn't know how to focus on my individual growth. The more I got hurt, the less I devoted. I was hurt emotionally and verbally so much that I fell out of love. Even though I was no longer in love, I still loved and cared about him. I felt as though I couldn't live without him. I believed, no one really wanted me for me, they were only interested in what I could do for them or how I made them feel. I was cute, but I wasn't that cute to be able to get any man I wanted, so I stayed. I began to feel trapped. I felt as though I failed God, my mom, and my family. Was I breaking the generational curse of abuse? Nope, not at all! It was just a different form of abuse that I wasn't used to seeing so I didn't even notice it when it was happening to me. This was such a burden that I didn't know how to get free from. I was brainwashed into thinking I was weak and couldn't live without him. I often ask myself now why didn't I leave sooner. I realize now that I never gave myself time to heal from my previous relationships and childhood pain. I was expecting him to make me happy. I didn't know who I was. I didn't love myself and because the relationships validated me as a woman, I felt like I needed to be in a relationship. I didn't need a man to take care of me, I just felt lonely not having companionship. I imagine that's how my mom felt. I've learned to be happy with me. Even though I still yearn for companionship, I no longer feel lonely or empty because I don't have a man. I'm focused on living life for me and building my relationship with God. I was once told, "He who finds a wife, finds a good thing. You just be the good thing". I'm working on being the good thing. I can see myself getting married again but this time doing it right. Knowing and loving myself so I can adequately love someone else. Also asking God for the foresight and discernment to see the least obvious within a person and be able to identify the one he has for me. I refuse to fall into the same trap again.

Just as I didn't have all the tools needed to have a perfect life, I'm sure my mom didn't. There is always something that will come along in life to test you and all along its building you up. My past relationships have opened my eyes. I see how low I thought of myself to allow someone to call me out my name, to steal from me and mistreat me. Open your eyes baby girl! I began to see my situation for what it was and not for what I hoped it to be. I stopped being focused on the potential, instead focused on the now and the current state of my relationship. I realized the change needed to start with me. I asked myself, how did I handle the depression and loneliness. How did I end up mirroring the same situation my mom endured? At first, I had no answer. I was so accustomed to just dealing with things and pushing through. I suppressed emotions because I didn't know how to express them in a positive way. I never considered how different emotions would affect my actions. At a young age, I started dating guys and was promiscuous. I felt wanted, desired and loved when a man would show me attention.

Once I got married, I felt like I was complete. I realized when the hurt and deceit started I no longer felt complete. I never did the inner soul work to make myself whole, complete and happy. I knew I had to make a change if I wanted to be happy. I had to do some self-reflection and pray to God asking him to reveal to me the things that were hindering my spiritual growth. I started to see how I was following the same path as my mom. I started ending toxic relationships, being conscious of my alone time and used it to strengthen my relationship with God through prayer, meditation, and worship. The alone time caused a shift in my emotional psyche. I no longer wanted to find my worth in a man; however, I was still stuck in a relationship that no longer uplifted me, only hindered me. I was still on my journey of healing and the person I was becoming did not mesh well with the person my spouse was used to. I wasn't drinking or partying. I didn't want to hang around certain people, doing certain things. I was on a path to follow the will of God for my life. Believe it or not, this caused a strain on our marriage and this is where we began to grow apart. I was building my relationship with God and started to realize who I was, what I was and what I wasn't going to accept. I decided I was worth more. Where there was doubt if I was breaking generational curses, there is only confidence. I break generational curses. I am who I say I am. I am who God says I am.

Chapter Five: The Vision

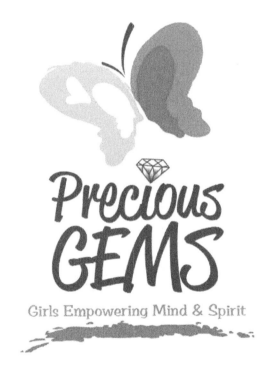

In the midst of my feelings of burden and lacking confidence, while in a destructive relationship, I started a nonprofit organization to empower young girls. Yep! I know you're thinking; how can you empower a child and you don't even believe in yourself? Well, that was my question too! At the age of 17, I got a vision from God of me standing in front of a large crowd and encouraging them. I also saw myself interacting and inspiring young girls. After the vision, I began to feel a passion in my heart to help empower girls. I was in no shape to empower anyone, so I thought. I ignored all those visions and signs God sent my way. At age 23 after I got married, those visions came back and the passion intensified. All I could think about was mentoring girls. I began to feel convicted. I felt like I was wrong for not wanting to do something God was telling me to do. I felt like I had a void in my life like I wasn't fulfilling my purpose or living up to my full potential. I couldn't sleep and when I did sleep, I constantly dreamt of seeing myself helping young girls. I knew I had to do something. After 3 years of constantly dreaming and having visions, I began to pray for God to give me a name if it was truly meant for me to do it.

One night I woke up out my sleep and all I could hear was Precious G.E.M.S. (Girls Empowering Mind and Spirit). I still didn't want to believe this was meant for me. During this time, I was shy, quiet and didn't even really like interacting with people at all. God had to make this vision as clear as possible to me if he wanted me to do this. I began to pray for another sign. One Sunday I went to church, my Pastor at the time, preached, "The pregnant plan of God." I knew then God was speaking to me. He said there was someone in the crowd that God had given a vision to and it's time now to bring that thing forth. You've been wondering when or how but God says now is the time. My Pastor had an altar call and I went up. Altar call is a moment in the worship service where you can go before the Lord and have the pastor pray with you. He prophesied to me and said, God was talking to me! He began to pray for me and all I could do was cry. I could hear a small voice saying, "If you start, I'll finish." I felt warm all over and a feeling of relief and confirmation. Even though I was nervous about what was to come, I was also excited. Immediately after church was over, I went to talk to my Pastor about all that I was experiencing. This experience was the fall of 2013. I did a year of research and by January 2014, at the age of 27, Precious G.E.M.S., Inc was BIRTHED.

I had no clue where to start or what to do. I just followed God's lead. The more I prayed and fasted, as my grandmother taught me, the more ideas were revealed to me. Also, the more I sought after God, I started to notice that he would send people my way that would help guide me in the right direction and teach me new things about operating a nonprofit organization. I was so scared and didn't know what to expect, but I was obedient to God and did what he gave me to do. I just recently heard someone say, you do what you can and let God do what you can't.

The day before the launch of my new nonprofit organization my husband was out and didn't come home. The next morning, the actual launch date, I found out he, my husband, had cheated. What a blow to my heart. I was already feeling underqualified for what I was about to do, and now all I wanted most was to curl up in my bed and cry. Instead, I had to do like I've done my entire life, take the punches and keep moving. Reflecting back, I had a lack of trust in God and in the abilities, He had given me. As Proverbs 3:5-6 says, "Trust in the Lord with all thine heart, and lean not unto thine own understanding. In all your ways acknowledge him, and he shall direct your path". I was trying but there was a lot of doubt. I went on that day in spite of my personal circumstances and actually enjoyed interacting with those young ladies. I knew then I had found my purpose. My goal for Precious GEMS is for us to always be able to provide a place where girls can grow, learn, have fun and develop confidence in themselves and their abilities to make a difference in their own lives and in the lives of others. We empower the mind and spirit of young girls through mentoring and teaching them the principles of support, responsibility, commitment, and possibility. I personally like to build relationships with each girl because I want them all to know that I'm there for them and genuinely want them to succeed. All of the hard life lessons I learned along the way are incorporated into the organization as a learning tool to inform a young lady to make better life choices.

Since I started the organization, I have grown and evolved into an even more powerful, strong and resilient woman. I have had many hurdles that should have taken me out and made me quit. Instead of being defeated I took each hurdle in stride and with each one learning who God is.

Chapter Six:

Midlife Journey

Being married, being the founder of a startup nonprofit organization, attending Old Dominion University as a full-time student with 14 credit hour classes and working full time as a surgical technologist on a demanding job in the operating room was very overwhelming. There were long nights in the library at school where I would use the computer and printer for research after doing homework or studying for an exam. I had no time for myself or family. I was on a new journey with many moving parts. I was 4 years into a marriage, still learning how to be a wife. It was my second year on my job and I was still learning. I was a student, learning how the entire body has an effect on speech. I was researching and starting a non-profit organization, which was a huge learning experience. I was also learning from God as I was trying to build my relationship with him. I didn't know how to balance everything that I had going on. Neither did I make time for God to lead and guide me in all areas of my life.

I have patience and trust issues that sometimes get in my way. When it came to my relationship, I didn't allow God to be the driver. If I wanted my husband to change, I felt like I had to make it known. I didn't allow God to do the changing. Needless to say, my relationship with my husband was strained. I was always busy. He built up resentment towards me because he felt as though I never made time for him, I wanted to change him into what I thought he should've been as a husband and there was constant fussing because of lies and cheating. So by the age of 30, we were divorced. I take full responsibility for the role I played in the events that led up to our divorce. I had no clue who I was. Do you see a pattern? Similar to my mom's relationship timeline. My identity was entangled within my husband and without him, I felt as though I didn't have value. Me not being a wife, made me feel not needed or not wanted. Those emotional demons that I didn't diligently work to devour reintroduced themselves in my life during my divorce. I didn't allow myself to become depressed. I did have some dark days. I just decided not to stay in those moments. My emotions were all over the place. I thought I was going to lose my mind. Some days I felt happy and free, I felt sad, angry, lonely, ugly and not good enough. All of this was taking place just when I thought I was at an age in my life where my confidence was better and overall, I felt better about myself. The divorce was a true testament of how far I had come with my self-worth. I was better, but I wasn't healed. The situations that led up to my divorce took me back to a dark place. I was questioning everything about myself again. There were days that I just cried alone in my apartment, not knowing which way to turn. I started to feel guilty, like it was all my fault.

I felt like I didn't know how to properly love him. My love was heartless. When I would get mad, I wouldn't talk to him or want him to touch me. I realize now, that was my way of thinking I could "control" him into doing what I thought he should or shouldn't do.

I was consumed with emotions. I felt lonely. I realized I went from years of sharing my life with someone to suddenly having no one to share it with. I fell right back into the trap of not wanting to be alone. Then, of course, I found false lustful love in the wrong person. We dated for 6 months, and I knew he wasn't the person I needed to be with, however, because I felt like I needed some type of companionship I just settled for the first person that found me attractive and made me feel good. I eventually got free from that "situationship". He was so similar to my ex-husband. They both were products of a broken home and were raised by grandparents. They had emotional damage that never healed from their childhood which manifested itself with insecurities, jealousy, rage, selfishness, lack of communication, and inability to be vulnerable. This new guy would disregard how I felt about anything, like I didn't even matter.

He knew I hated the smell of cigarette smoke. One day he decides to get in my car with his freshly lit newport 100 cigarette. I expressed to him, that he had to put that out because he couldn't smoke in my car and he ignores me. I started arguing which made him mad and caused him to be even more stubborn. He continued to ignore me and kept smoking the cigarette. I felt like I was repeating the same relationship with a different person. I was with someone who didn't truly love me nor did I truly love him, we were just going through the motions of fulfilling our yearning for companionship. When I look back, I realize we both were hurting. He was a drug dealer, with no job, no car and was struggling to get back on track. The typical "street dude", who had a million so call friends but no real friends to be there when he needed them. He had just got out of a relationship just as I did. We both were looking for love to heal our pain.

I had a reality check, and I knew I didn't want to keep following down the same path, making the same mistakes. I could feel myself starting to fall for him. I began to dwell on my mom's life. I had fallen into the generational curse again and didn't even know I was consumed by it. I had to change. I was tired of the cycle. I didn't want to be silenced by shame or end up dead, unable to tell my truth to save someone else or encourage someone. I decided to focus on me and figure out who I was as a person. Being in a relationship since 16 years old, you tend to lose your identity. I never had the chance to learn who I was or what I wanted without having to consider how it would affect someone else's life.

I vowed to myself and God to be celibate and focus on his purpose for my life. Celibacy was hard at first. I even had a few hiccups along the way. I had been sexually active since 16 years old and then at 30, was deciding to make a lifestyle change. Only when I changed my mindset did it become easier. Every time I fell for temptation and would have sex I felt so condemned and unsatisfied. I got tired of feeling like I was letting my flesh win. I had to start believing that my body was precious and I was worth more than a hot second screw. My goal was to figure out what lessons I was supposed to learn from my marriage, divorce and all the highs and lows in between. I needed to figure out what was God's ultimate purpose and plan for my life. I went back to my roots.... fasting and praying. I went on a 21 day fast. During the 21 days, I ate only fruits, vegetables, natural juices, and water. I also spent my mornings before work and nights before bed in meditation, prayer, and worship. I also did a lot of self-reflection, thinking about how I could make changes to become a better person. How did I get to this place in my life? Why was this happening to me? Why do bad things keep happening to me? Another time in my life I felt like Job. Those 21 days revealed many things to me, spiritually and naturally. Many tears were shed during this time. I felt like I was on an emotional roller coaster. There were days that I felt so free because I decided to be strong and decided to love me more. Then there were days that I felt so empty with nothing else to give anyone. I continued to push through with the fast, continued to worship and pray. I learned that a man doesn't define who I am, that's something I create. I learned that people will only do what you allow them to do to you. I've heard that all my life but during the fast, it clicked for me. I have to carry myself in a way that demands respect. No form of disrespect should be tolerated however there is a way to correct in love and not out of anger.

Most importantly I learned to love EVERYTHING about me. If I don't love myself then no one can properly love me. I learned to live and enjoy every moment in life because life is short. Your situation can change in the blink of an eye for good or bad. I learned that I can be controlling and may not handle all situations with love. When I'm angry I can use words that cut deep. I have learned patience and every day I'm diligently working towards a better me. God created me for greatness. I now know that I can't be attached to anything or just anybody. Usually, people dread being 30 years old. In my case turning 30 did start off rough but it became a midlife journey of me learning who I was and experiencing things I had never experienced before. I started to travel more with friends and meet new people. I started living my life to the fullest and enjoying learning about what I liked and how I felt about myself. All the negative things I let them go. I have moments like everyone when I think on some of the bad things that happen in my life and I realize I've been on a journey. Any interesting adventurous journey has peaks and valleys.

Chapter Seven:
Freedom and Growth

I'm 31 years old and I'm living my best life. I'm the happiest I've ever been. Of course, everything in my life isn't perfect. I still deal with some of the same things other women deal with, bills, debt, bad days at work, wanting attention or yearning for companionship. However, my outlook on life is completely different now. My mindset has changed. Even though I'm alone, I no longer feel lonely anymore. I travel the world, meet new people, and also started a new job where I get to travel all over the world if I chose to. I'm grateful for all the new experiences I have allowed myself to be a part of. I have learned how to love myself and enjoy focusing on me instead of trying to fulfill someone else's needs and desires. I feel free! I'm free to just be the me that God created. When I focused on my own individual purpose in life, is when I began to grow. I've grown spiritually, naturally, mentally and financially. I wake up every day with the intentions of having a great day. Regardless of what is said or done throughout the day, I smile. I have gone through too much in my life to allow the small things to bring me down. It took some time but growth and freedom made me realize how to live my life to its full potential. My scars don't represent defeat, they represent my victory. I've learned that if you wait until something good happens to be happy then you will never be happy. You have to stop waiting for your happiness and create it. Keep joy in your heart and be intentional throughout your day to show joy and create positive vibes. Where there is joy, there is happiness. God has taken me away from my issues but he has not removed the issues from me. They are a reminder of how far I've come and that I'll always need God to keep me on track.

Chapter Eight:
Faith Walk

Faith without works is dead. Works without faith is dead. You can't have one without the other. I've just recently grasped the true understanding of that scripture. I know the Lord will make a way for me. I just have to do my part and do the work. I used to believe and pray for my change. Now I realize that my change starts with me. I have to believe and trust that God will make a way, that he'll lead and guide me but I also must put in some work to reach my goals. I was sad all the time but wanted to be happy. I learned to make conscious decisions to do things that made me happy. I shouldn't rely on someone else for my happiness.

My life could have turned out to be completely different. However, I knew when I was only 10 years old, I did not want my life to be like my environment. I diligently worked at being successful. I am still striving for better. I have enough faith to believe that everything I desire, I will have. I have a determined mind and with God strengthening me, ALL things are possible. I refuse to become a product of my surroundings.

I grew up with so many emotional and self-esteem issues. I endured emotional abusive relationships. I had to learn life's lessons the hard way. I have also had many loved ones to pass away. Six close relatives died within four years. My father, with whom I just started to build a relationship, died December 2010. My father was not in my life as a child. The first time we met, I was 8 years old. He was very well known. Everybody knew he was not to be messed with or anyone he cared about. He was a bounty hunter and was good at his job. He was the popular, well known aggressive bounty hunter and an alcoholic. I can literally count on one hand how many times we briefly saw each other. With each time we met, I remember the stench of liquor rising out of his pours. I never had much respect for him because he was never a man of his word. He would always say he's going to do something for me or come see me and he wouldn't show up. Even though I knew his M.O. I still wanted to give him another chance to show me he cared. June 2010 I called and invited my dad to my wedding. During this call I found out he had cirrhosis of the liver. Cirrhosis is scarring on the liver caused by hepatitis or chronic alcoholism. Due to the stage it was in, he wasn't eligible for a liver transplant. To my surprise he showed up at my wedding July 3, 2010. A yearning to bond with him was sparked. He started to call to check on me regularly and was interested in getting some of my wedding pictures. We were finally starting to build a father/daughter relationship. 5 months after my wedding he passed away. Then 5 months after my dad died my grandfather died May

2011, 3 months later my best friend since kindergarten died August 2011 at the age of 24, my Aunt Ann (on my dad side) died January 2013. I was closer to her than anyone on my dad's side. She always was there to support me and just popped up and visited me whenever she wanted. My grandmother died Feb 2014 and my mother in law died June 2014. All that grief was very difficult to deal with. I felt like I couldn't catch a break. Only the grace of God brought me through that. When my grandfather and best friend died 3 months apart, I felt like my heart was breaking. I couldn't eat or sleep. I miss all my loved ones dearly. Grief is never an easy thing to deal with, however, I continued to cry out to God to strengthen me. I always have a void in my heart for those people that I love so dearly. Even through all the pain yet I still smile. Without God, I would not be the person I am today or be on the level I am mentally and spiritually. My faith was tested through each journey. My faith has increased because God has shown himself worthy and has never left me nor forsaken me, even in the times it felt like he wasn't there.

I walk by faith and not by sight. Things in my life have been hard and I still continue to have challenges because I'm determined to not stay in my comfort zone. In order to grow, you have to be stretched, meaning there will be trials, errors, and situations you think you are not built for. However, you must overcome your fears. God did not give us the spirit of fear. Faith your fears! Show your fears how BIG your God is and put some action towards working on your goals in life or just working on improving your inner being. Faith Walk your journey and I guarantee you will succeed. God's word says he has a plan to see you prosper and give you an expected end. Trust in him with all your heart and lean not to your own understanding. I now know to whom I belong and his hands are always wide open to embrace me and the love that I was searching for, I found in him. Finding love in God, made me love myself. How could you not love such a wonderful creation, God created us in his image. I can truly say, I have found fulfillment in Christ.

How to Transition Into the YOU, You Didn't Know

1. Identify the Problem. You can't fix what you don't know is broken. If it's a destructive relationship, generational curses, low self-esteem, self-love issues, anger/temper, etc. Identify what needs to be changed.

2. Once the problem is identified, take the necessary steps to change your situation. End detrimental relationships, whether it's spouse/partner, friends or family. Sacrifice getting out of your comfort zone to focus on developing the love for yourself.

3. Build or strengthen your relationship with God. Begin to worship and praise God for the things you believe but don't yet see happening and may not even see how it will happen. Set aside an appointed time to be alone in the presence of God. Take this time to meditate, pray, worship, praise God and/or read his word. Get to know God on an intimate level.

4. Start Self-Reflecting and write down the things you want to change about your inner/outer self. If you want peace of mind, love in your heart, the ability to forgive, confidence in yourself, or the ability to face your fears, etc. write it down so you can visually see all the things that need to be

changed. The Bible says in Habakkuk 2:2 to write the vision and make it plain.

5. Set goals for yourself to accomplish the things you want to be changed. Start applying to jobs you've always wanted but felt as though you were not qualified. Start that new business you've been dreaming of. Whatever you want to be changed in your life, be proactive about creating that change...CHANGE STARTS WITH YOU!

6. Move with Swiftness and Confidence. As they say, "Fake it until you make it". Whatever strategies you come up with to provoke change, just do it like NIKE. Act upon it with swiftness before you allow fear to put

doubt in your heart and mind. Be confident in God and in the abilities, He has given you.

7. Have Down Time. As you start to change, everything around you will change. People you thought would be in your corner and support you may turn their backs on you. You will meet new people who will help push you into your purpose. During this time, it's important to take time out for yourself to refocus and clear your mind. You can't be STRONG for others and neglect to take care of yourself. Even if it's just a pampering day, go get a mani/pedi, invest in yourself.

8. When temptation comes or situations arise to take you back to where you have

evolved from, immediately analyze it and see it for what it truly is and don't allow yourself to fall for the trap. However, If you do fall, don't stay down. You must quickly get up, brush yourself off and repent to God for any wrongdoings and then keep pushing. The devil's only job is to kill, steal and destroy. He'll do it by any means necessary. Stay on alert and constantly remind yourself that you're worthy of greatness.

9. Once you've found yourself and have started to walk into your true purpose, help someone else. Be a living testimony.

10. Last but most certainly not least, always give God glory. As my grandmother would

say, "When I look back over my life and I think things over, I can truly say I got a testimony". Never forget where your help lies and your strength comes from. Its ok to look back in your past to encourage yourself that you may not be what you want to be but you're nowhere near where you used to be.

About the Author

When Devona Natalie Boone was just 10 years old, she witnessed her mother's murder. Eunice Natalie Boone was stabbed multiple times by an abusive boyfriend while Devona watched in extreme fear. Devona was with her mother until her very last breath. After the tragedy, Devona was overcome with sadness, worry, and grief and she was unsure of what was next for her.

Despite her circumstances, Devona graduated high school with honors and earned a Bachelor's Degree in Communicative Science Disorders with a minor in Special Education in 2014.

Throughout her life, Devona has met every challenge with hard work, dedication, and faith.

If you talk to her today she will tell you that she is blessed beyond measure. Her goal in life is to provide young girls with a support system filled with love, guidance and understanding. Through her faith in God and with the support of her family, she excels at everything she does.

You can find out more about Devona's story at
www.AuthorDevonaBoone.com
You can also follow her on all social media platforms at
@AuthorDevonaBoone

Made in the USA
Columbia, SC
27 March 2021